SMART BRAIN RIGHT BRAIN

Telling Time

Om KIDZ
An imprint of Om Books International

First Published in 2021 by

Om Kidz | Om Books International

Corporate & Editorial Office
A-12, Sector 64, Noida 201 301
Uttar Pradesh, India
Phone: +91 120 477 4100
Email: editorial@ombooks.com
Website: www.ombooksinternational.com

Sales Office
107, Ansari Road, Darya Ganj
New Delhi 110 002, India
Phone: +91 11 4000 9000
Email: sales@ombooks.com

Author: Shweta Sinha
Editor: Kirti Pathak
Art & Design: Anshuman Pandey, Gaurav Bhandari, Harish Arya

ISBN: 978-93-5276-859-2

Printed in India

10 9 8 7 6 5 4 3 2 1

CONTENTS

1.	Day and Night	4
2.	Lengths of Time	6
3.	Time Measuring Devices	8
4.	Telling the Time	12
5.	Quarter Past and Quarter To	18
6.	Time in Numbers	22
7.	The Time Gone By	24
	Let's Get Active	28
	Glossary	32
	Answers	32

1. Day and Night

Daytime is when the Sun is out in the sky and its light and heat can reach you. Night time is when the Sun has set and is shining on the other side of the Earth. At night the sky is dark, the Sun's light and heat cannot reach you, and you can see the stars and the moon.

We get day and night because the Earth spins on an imaginary line called an Axis, which makes different parts of the planet face the Sun at different times. The time of day changes as the Sun moves across the sky. Your daily routine and activities depend upon what time of the day it is.

I do different things at different times of the day.

Morning:
I wake up. I bathe and have my breakfast.

Afternoon:
I have my lunch.

Night:
I have dinner. I go to bed.

Evening:
I go outside to play with my friends.

POCKET FACT

When it is daytime for you, it is night time for someone else in another part of the world.

Times of the Day

Different times of the day and the night are known by different names. The names vary with the movement of the Sun and the moon in the sky.

Noon/Midday
12 o' clock at daytime

Dawn
at sunrise

Dusk
at sunset

Midnight
12 o'clock night time

DID YOU KNOW?

Noon is 12 o' clock in the daytime whereas midnight is 12 o' clock in the night time.

2. Lengths of Time

We use hours, minutes and seconds to measure time.

Second- Speaking the words 'one thousand' takes just one second.

Minute- 60 seconds make one minute. It takes a minute to brush your teeth.

Hour- 60 minutes make one hour. It takes about an hour to bake a cake.

Day- 24 hours make a day. It takes the Earth 24 hours to go all the way round its axis.

The 24 hours of a day are split into two parts - AM and PM. Each part is 12 hours long. We use AM to tell the time running from midnight until noon and PM for time running from noon until midnight.

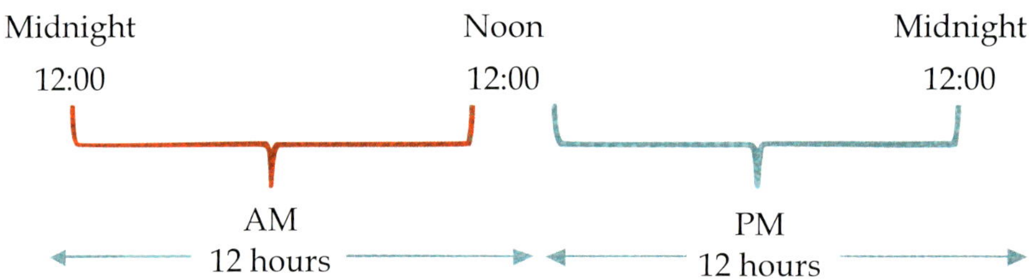

POCKET FACT The length of daytime changes over the year with the season. Days are longer in summer than in winter.

Units of Time Conversions

60 seconds = 1 minute

60 minutes = 1 hour

24 hours = 1 day

7 days = 1 week

52 weeks = 1 year

365 days = 1 year

Decade = 10 years

Century = 100 years

Millennium = 1,000 years

Using the above conversion chart, you can easily convert hours into minutes and minutes into seconds. So, to convert hours into minutes, multiply the hour by 60.

2 hours = 2 × 60 minutes = 120 minutes.

3 hours = 3 × 60 minutes = 180 minutes.

Similarly, to convert minutes into seconds, multiply the minutes by 60.

5 minutes = 5 × 60 seconds = 300 seconds.

Quiz

Can you find out how many minutes and seconds are there in a day?

Answer:

1 day = 24 hours = 24 × 60 minutes = 1,440 minutes.

1,440 minutes = 1440 × 60 seconds = 86,400 seconds.

3. Time Measuring Devices

Sundial

A sundial is an old form of clock that uses the shadows cast by the Sun to tell time. Sundials tracked the passing of time during the day only. And if the day was cloudy, they wouldn't work at all.

At different times of the day, the Sun casts shadows on different parts of the dial, indicating the time.

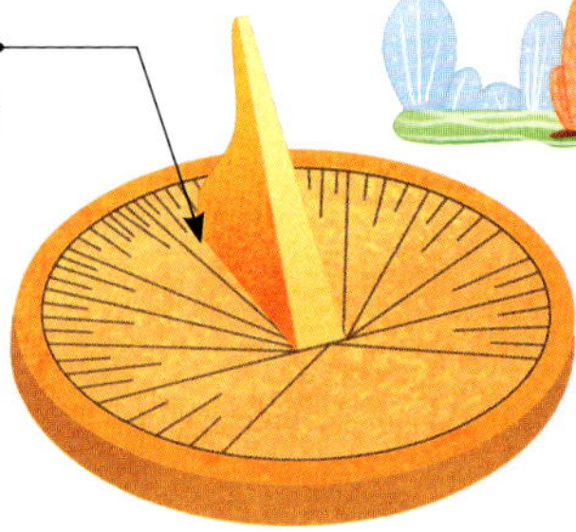

Hourglass

An hourglass only measures the elapsed time or the duration.

The flow of sand trickling slowly is used to measure the elapsed time.

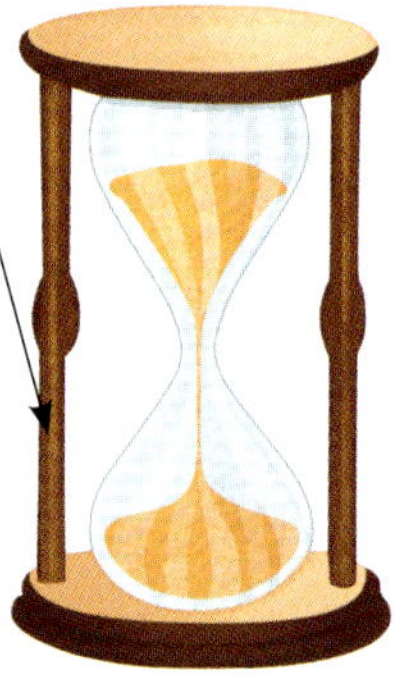

Analogue Clock

A clock with numbers and hands is an analogue clock. We use analogue clocks to measure time duration and to tell time. The clock face shows the numbers from 1 to 12. Hands on the clock move along the numbers to indicate the time. The long hand points to the minutes. The little hand points to the hours. Some clocks have a third hand that is thinner than the other two. This is the seconds hand and it moves much faster than the minute or the hour hands.

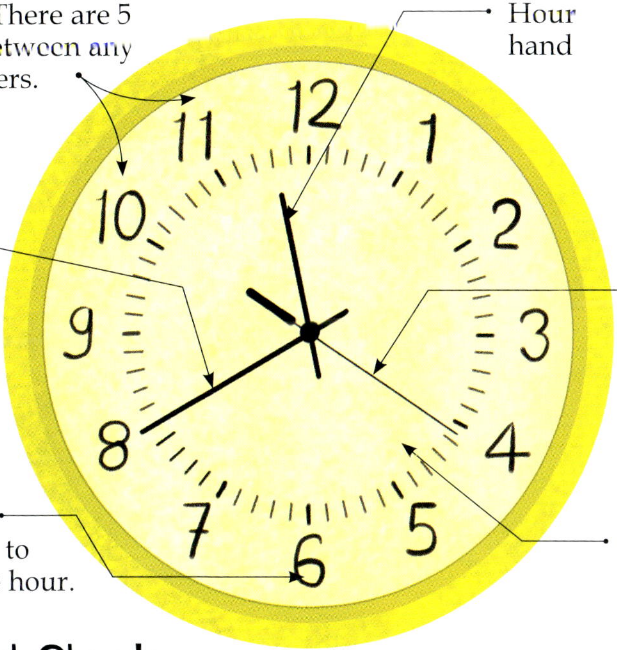

Digital Clock

Digital clocks use numbers and a colon symbol (:) to display the time. They are usually easier to read than analogue clocks. They are also smaller in size. Some modern digital clocks can even correct themselves using the internet.

DID YOU KNOW?

Atomic clocks are the most accurate clocks in the world. They use electromagnetic waves to measure time.

12-Hour Clock

Even though a day has 24 hours, we often describe time using a 12-hour clock. The hours hand on a 12-hour clock goes from one o' clock in the night to twelve o' clock at noon. The cycle then repeats from one o' clock in the afternoon to twelve o' clock midnight.

1.00 pm - 4.00 pm
At school or studying
at home.

5:00 pm - 7:00 pm
Watching TV and
Playing with friends.

8:00 pm
Dinner time

9:00 pm
Bedtime

We use p.m. (pm) to
show time after noon.

Midnight (12:00 am)

DID YOU KNOW?

The calendar date changes at the stroke of midnight. Sunday changes to Monday, Monday to Tuesday and so on, every night at 12:00 am.

4. Telling the Time

An analogue clock is a 12-hour clock. Each day, the hour hand moves twice across an analogue clock – once from midnight to noon in 12 hours and again from noon to midnight in another 12 hours. This makes one full day of 24 hours.

The hour hand takes 1 hour to move from one number to the next.

The minute hand takes 5 minutes to move from one number to the next. The hand takes 30 minutes to move half-way across the clock and 60 minutes to make one full circle.

Now, 60 minutes = 1 hour

So, every hour the minute hand moves once across the clock.

The minute hand takes 1 hour to go around the clock once.

POCKET FACT A wristwatch is a small clock that you can wear on your wrist. It can be either analogue or digital.

What is the Hour?

To tell time, look at the little hand first. When the little hand is pointing directly at a number it is on the hour. Express the time as the **number o' clock.**

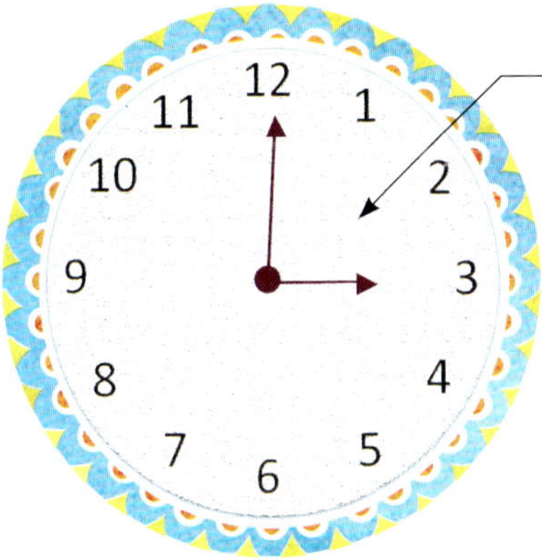

The hour hand is pointing directly at the number 3. The time is exactly **3 o' clock.**

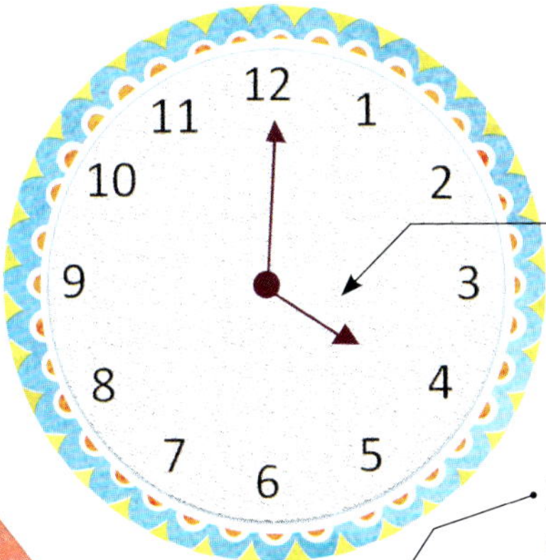

The hour hand is pointing directly at the number 4. The time is exactly **4 o' clock.**

Notice that the minute hand points directly at 12. It means there are no minutes. Hence, the number that the hour hand points at shows full hours.

Quiz

Here both hands are pointing at 12. Can you tell the time?

Answer: 12 o' clock.

Minutes Past

There are little lines in between two numbers. These mark the minutes. The minute hand takes 1 minute to move from one line to the next. The hour hand also moves with the minute hand, but at a much slower pace.

The lines at the numbers are longer or darker to make it easier to read the hours.

A clock has 60 little lines in total across its face. They indicate 60 minutes.

What is the time when the hour hand is in between numbers?

Look at the number the hour hand has just crossed and the number where the minute hand is pointing at to get the time.

The hour hand is in between 3 and 4. As it has not yet reached 4, it is not yet 4 o c'clock. The hour is still 3.

The minute hand is also not pointing at number 12.

Counting minutes

1. If the minute hand is pointing directly at a number, add five minutes for every number the minute hand has passed after 12.

Or, minutes passed = number × 5

The minute hand is pointing at 5. So minutes passed = 5×5, which is 25 minutes.

Hour =3 and Minutes = 25. Hence the time is **25 minutes past 3**.

2. If the minute hand is not directly pointing at a number

(a) Look at the last number the minute hand just crossed. Multiply that number by 5 as before.

(b) Then count the number of lines after the last number where the minute hand is pointing.

(c) Add both the numbers from a) and b) to get the minutes passed.

The minute hand has passed 5, and is pointing at the 2nd line after 5.

So, minute = (5×5)+2

Hour =3

Minutes = 25 + 2 = 27 minutes

Hence the time is 27 minutes past 3.

Quiz

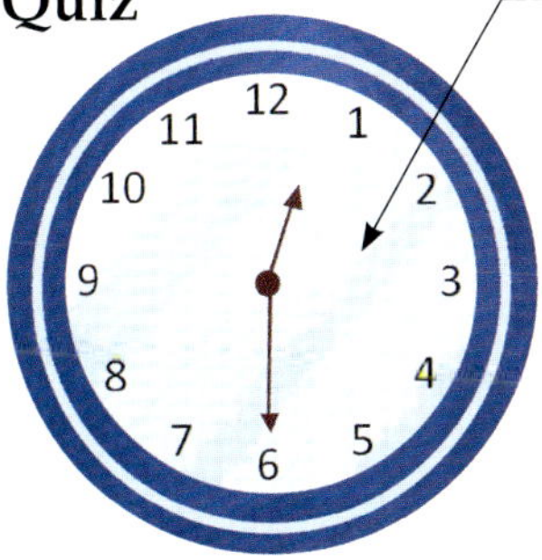

The hour hand is in between 12 and 1 and the minute hand is pointing at 6. Can you tell the time?

Answer:

Time = 30 minutes past 12

To the Hour

Once the minute hand has moved more than halfway around the clock, you can tell the time by counting how many minutes are remaining until the next o' clock.

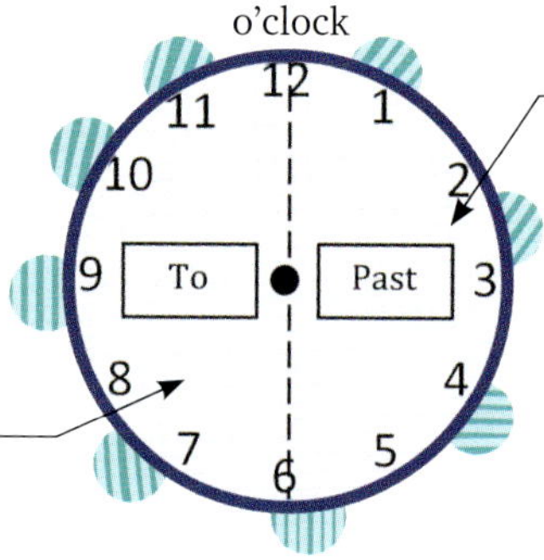

If the minute hand is on this side, count **Past.**

If the minute hand is on this side, count **To**

When the minute hand has moved more than half way around the clock, look at the number the hour hand is about to reach. Always count the hours and minutes in the direction the hands move.

The minute hand is at 11. So, 5 minutes are left for it to reach 12.

The hour hand is about to reach 4.

The time shown by this clock is **5 minutes to 4.**

Quiz

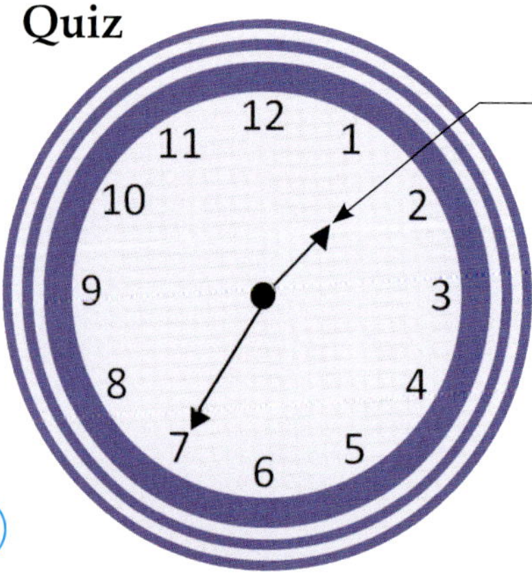

The hour hand is about to reach 2 and the minute hand is pointing at 7. Can you tell the time?

Answer: The minute hand will take 25 minutes to reach 12. So, time = 25 minutes to 2.

Onto the Next Hour

As the minute hand moves around the clock, it finally reaches 12 once again. This marks the 60th minute. The hour hand moves to the next number and the minutes is reset to 0.

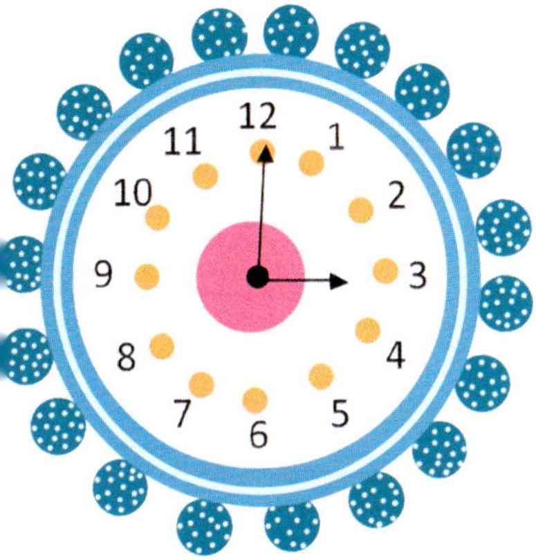

3 o'clock

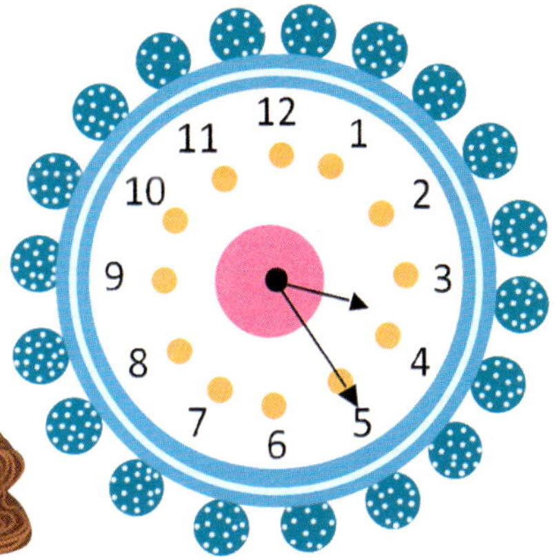

25 minutes past 3

5 minutes to 4

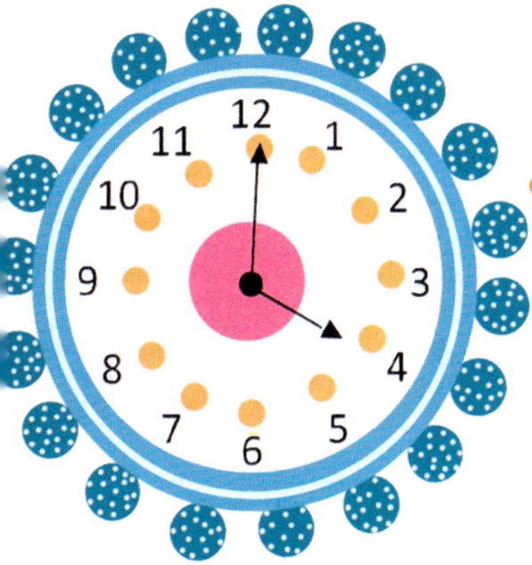

The minutes hand has reached 12 and the hour hand moves to 4. It is now 4 o' clock.

POCKET FACT

The hands of a clock always move in the same direction called as clockwise.

5. Quarter Past and Quarter To

You can divide an hour into four equal parts. Each part is known as a quarter.

A quarter hour is a period of **15 minutes** and is often used to tell time.

Every day

I wake up at **quarter past** seven.

I have my breakfast at **quarter to** eight.

I reach school at eight o' clock.

POCKET FACT

When the minute hand covers the first quarter from 12, it is **quarter past**. When the minute hand covers the first three-quarters from 12, it is **quarter to**.

Quarter Past

The first quarter lies at number 3. When the minute hand points to 3, it is quarter past the hour. It means 15 minutes have passed after 12. Look at the hour hand to find out the number it has just crossed. Tell the time as quarter past the hour.

The sun rises around **quarter past six**.

I eat my lunch around **quarter past noon.**

I do my homework at **quarter past three**.

I play with my friends at **quarter past five**.

It is my bedtime at **quarter past eight.**

I am fast asleep in bed at **quarter past midnight**.

Quarter To

When the minute hand points at 9, it is quarter to the hour. This means that only a quarter (15 minutes) is left to complete the hour. Look at the hour hand to find the number it is about to reach next. Tell the time as quarter to the hour.

Dad returns from his morning run at **quarter to seven**.

Mom leaves for work at **quarter to nine**.

I come home from school **at quarter to two**.

The sun sets around **quarter to six**.

We eat dinner at **quarter to eight**.

I am fast asleep in bed at **quarter to three** at night.

POCKET FACT

Quarter to the hour is the same as saying 15 minutes to the hour.

Half-Past

Just like quarters, you can use 'half-past' to tell time. Half past means thirty minutes past the hour. When the minute hand points at 6, it is half past the hour. Look at the hour hand to find out the number it has just crossed. Tell the time as half past the hour.

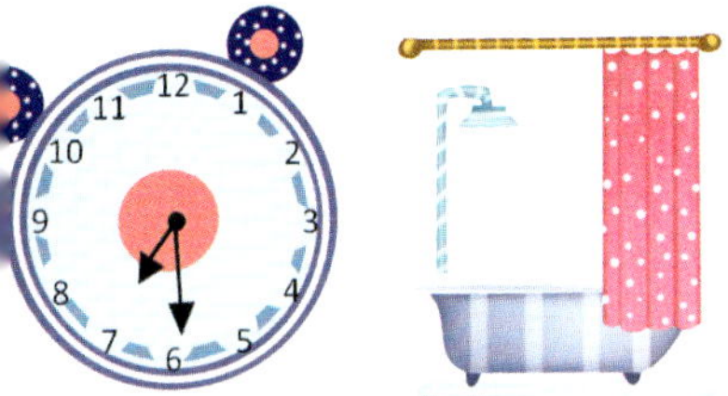

I take a shower at **half past seven**.

I am busy with my lessons at school at **half past ten**.

My favourite TV show starts at **half past four**.

I take piano lessons on Sundays at **half past five**.

Quiz

What is the correct order in which the times shown on these clocks occur?

1.

2.

3.

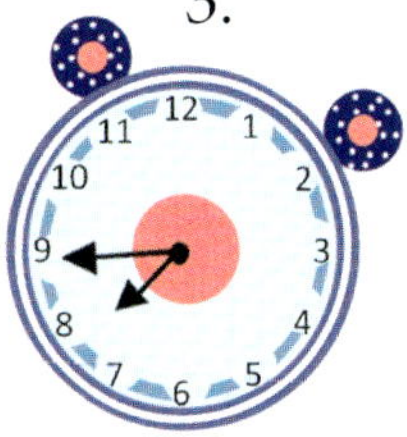

Answer:

(2) Quarter past seven; (1) Half past seven; (3) Quarter to eight

6. Time in Numbers

Time can also be expressed using numbers separated by a colon (:). The time on the clock below is 10 o′ clock. You can write this time in numbers as shown:

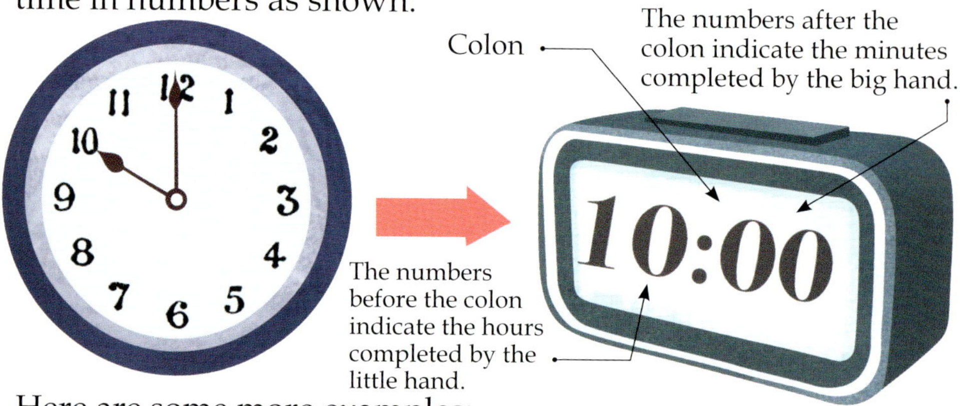

Here are some more examples:

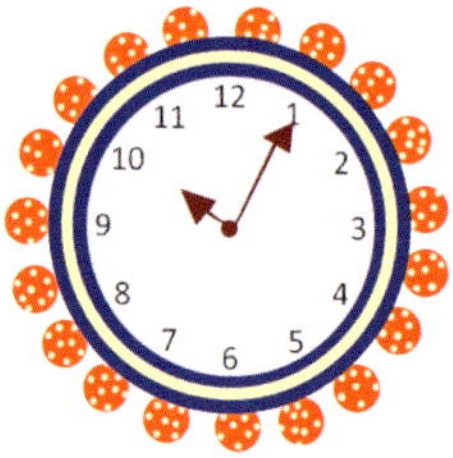

5 minutes past 10 = 10:05

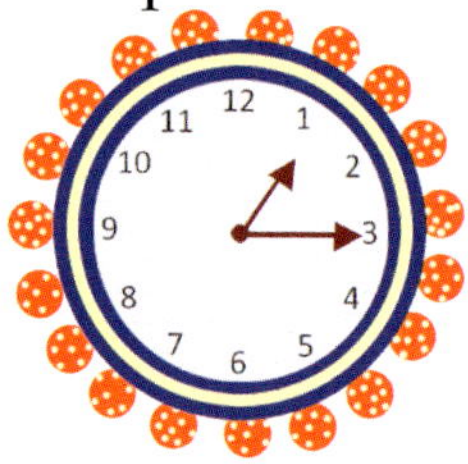

Quarter past 1 = 1:15

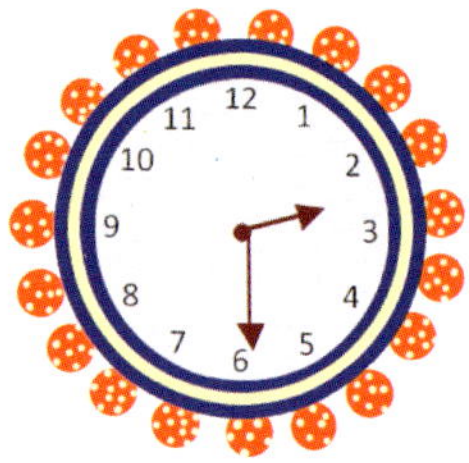

Half past 2 = 2:30

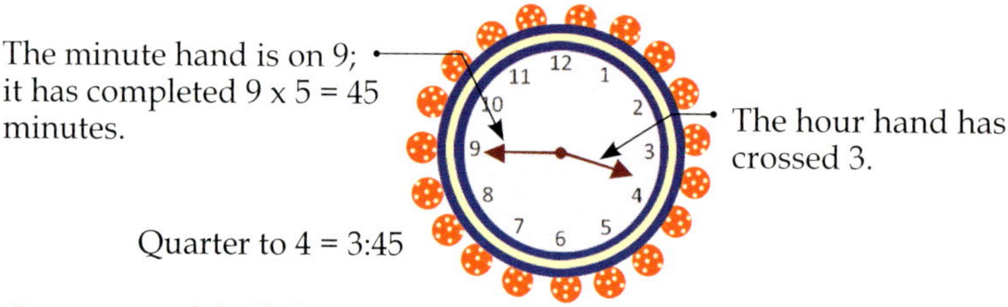

Quarter to 4 = 3:45

In case of full hours, it is necessary to show two zeroes after the colon.

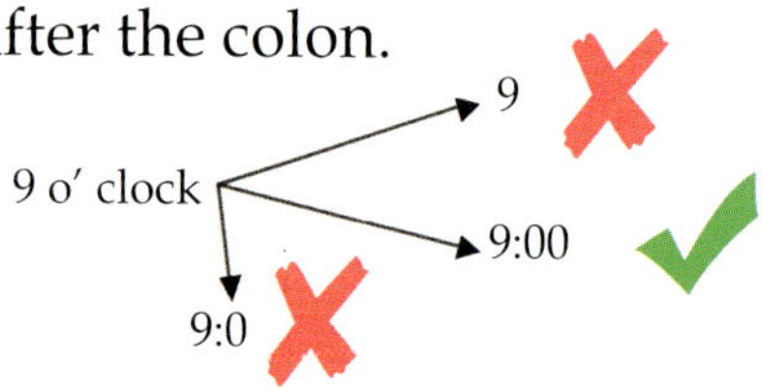

DID YOU KNOW?

A digital clock displays time using numbers separated by a colon.

AM and PM

Rosie's alarm clock woke her up at 7:00. Does this tell you if it woke her up at 7 o' clock in the morning or at 7 o' clock in the evening?

It is important to know which part of the day the time indicates. By adding 'am' or 'pm' to time, you can clearly tell whether the time occurs in the morning, afternoon or night. So, while 7:00 am occurs in the morning, 7:00 pm occurs in the evening.

Rosie's alarm clock woke her up at 7:00 am, which is 7 o' clock in the morning.

'am' stands for Ante Meridiem, and 'pm' stands for Post Meridiem. These are Latin terms that mean 'before noon' and 'after noon', respectively.

POCKET FACT

Midnight is written as 12:00 am, and noon is written as 12:00 pm.

7. The Time Gone By

Suppose you visited an amusement park. You reached there at 10:00 am. By the time you left, it was 3:00 pm. How much time did you spend at the amusement park?

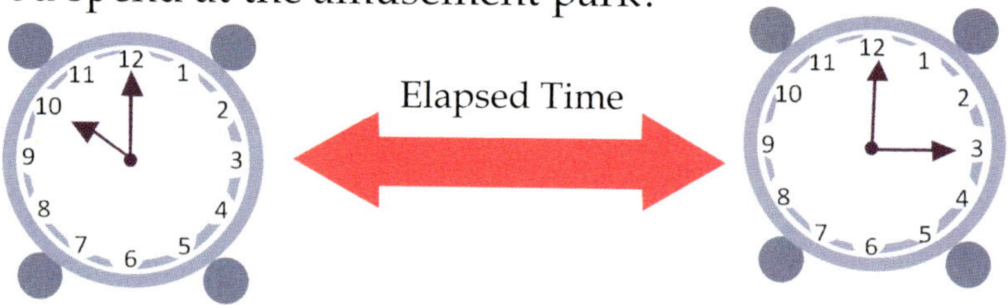

Start Time
(10:00 am)

End Time
(3:00 pm)

The amount of time that passes from the start time of an event to the end time is known as the elapsed time.

Elapsed Time with full hours

Start time = 10:00 am and End time = 3:00 pm

Both the start and end times are full hours. Use a clock to count the number of hours between the two times.

5 numbers are marked on the clock after 10 until the number 3. So, there are 5 hours between 10:00 am and 3:00 pm

POCKET FACT

If there are 5 hours between 10:00 am and 3:00 pm, there will be 5 hours between 10:00 pm and 3:00 am as well.

Elapsed time using a T-chart

When the start and end times have hours as well as minutes, it is not easy to count the elapsed time on a clock. You can use the T-chart method to calculate the elapsed time.

Step 1. Draw three columns on a sheet of ruled paper. Write down the start and end times on top of the chart for reference.

Start Time	End Time	Elapsed Time
9.44 am	2:47 pm	

Start time in the left-most column

End time in the middle column

Step 2. In the next row, once again write down the start time in the first column. Write a new end time depending on the amount of elapsed time you wish to work with at once.

Start Time	End Time	Elapsed Time
9:44 am	2:47 pm	
9:44 am	10:00 am	16 min

Original start time

New end time

Elapsed time

Step 3. The next start time is the same as your previous end time. You can increase or decrease the elapsed time you want to work with.

Start Time	End Time	Elapsed Time
9:44 am	2:47 pm	
9:44 am	10:00 am	16 min
10:00 am	11:00 am	1 hour

New start time = Previous end time

Different Elapsed times

Step 4. Continue until the end time matches the end time at the top of the chart.

Start Time	End Time	Elapsed Time
9:44 am	2:47 pm	
9:44 am	10:00 am	16 min
10:00 am	11:00 am	1 hour
11:00 am	12:00 pm	1 hour
12:00 pm	2:00 pm	2 hours
2:00 pm	2:47 pm	47 mins

Step 5. Sum up the elapsed times you have written on your chart. Add the hours and minutes separately.

Elapsed Time	
	16 min
1 hour	
1 hour	
2 hours	
	47 mins
4 hours	63 mins

If the sum of elapsed minutes > 60, convert the minutes into whole hours first.

Converting minutes to hours

To convert the minutes into whole hours, divide it by 60. The quotient of the division will be the hour and the remainder gives you the minutes.

So, 63 minutes/60 = 1 hour 3 minutes.

Elapsed Time

Now add the whole hour calculated above to the elapsed hour from step 5 = 4 + 1 hour = 5 hours

Minutes as calculated above = 3 minutes

Hence, Elapsed time = **5 hours 3 minutes**

Quiz

In a city in Finland, the sun rose at 11:00 am and set at 4:30 pm one winter day. How long was the daytime?

Answer: The daytime was 5 hours 30 minutes long.

When does it happen?

Match the pictures to the correct time when it happens.

1. 	(a) Dawn
2. 	(b) 7:45 am
3. 	(c) 9:30 pm
4. 	(d) 10:00 am
5. 	(e) Noon

Telling Time

Write the time shown by the clocks.

1. 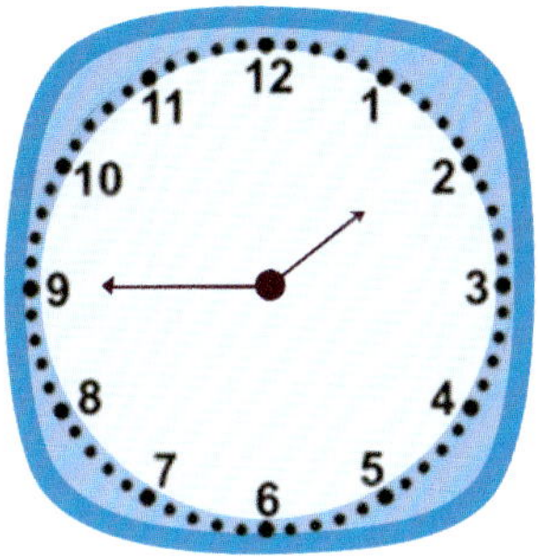

____

2. 

____

3. 

____

4. 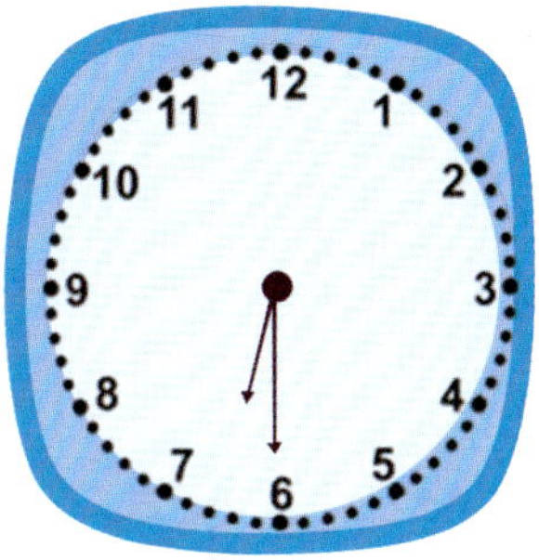

____

5. 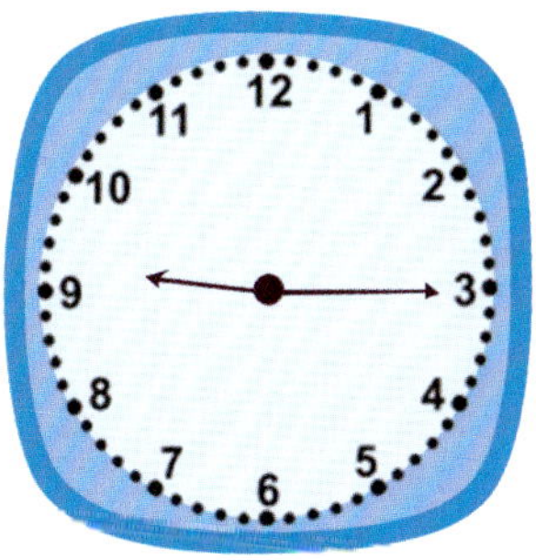

____

6. 

____

Show the Time

Draw hour and the minute hands on the clocks to show the time as mentioned.

1.

6:30

2.

5:00

3.

7:30

4.

10:30

5.

9:00

6.

6:00

Elapsed Time

Sean's flight takes off from London at 10:10 am and lands at Manchester at 11:20 am. Calculate the time duration of the flight.

Start Time	End Time	Elapsed Time
10:10 am	11:20 am	

Elapsed Time = ________ hours ________ minutes

GLOSSARY

Analogue clock	showing the time by means of hands or a pointer
Calculate	determine the amount or number of something mathematically.
Calendar	a chart or series of pages showing the days, weeks, and months of a particular year
Digital	involving or relating to the use of computer technology
Divide	separate or be separated into parts
Electromagnetic	relating to the interrelation of electric currents or fields and magnetic fields
Express	say or otherwise communicate what one thinks or means
Full hour	time with no or zero minute part
Internet	many computers that are connected like a web so you can see what other computer operators show you and you can show them things as well.
Latin	the language of ancient Rome and its empire
Measurement	a unit or system of measuring
Method	a particular procedure for accomplishing or approaching something,
Reference	to mention something
Reset	to set again or differently

ANSWERS

Page 28. 1. (c) 2. (e)
3. (a) 4. (b)
5. (d)

Page 29. (1) Quarter to two (2) Eight o' clock (3) Half past two (4) Half past six
(5) Quarter past nine
(6) Quarter past eight

Page 31. Elapsed Time = 1 hour 10 minutes